Note to Parents

1) Most of the activities in this book shoulc
appropriate developmental level, which w
to do them independently. But don't hesitate to
When parents are involved in the learning process, it increases a child's intellectual curiosity and creates a more effective, supportive learning environment.

2) To support your child's learning, review the **"To Parents"** section featured below the instructions. These tips offer parents effective ways to explain the activity to your child.

3) As mentioned on the previous page, this book is divided into three steps. Depending on the ability of your child, start with pages that they can handle and work up to the more difficult ones after a while. Some activities return to an earlier level of difficulty, and these will help strengthen your child's scissor-handling skills. If your child still has difficulty using the scissors, you can show them how to use the scissors by example.

Another feature of this book is that you can enjoy the illustrations on the back side of the pages. The back side of each page also has pictures, cutting lines, and starting marks for the scissors, so if your child is left-handed, they can look at the pictures on the back side and cut.

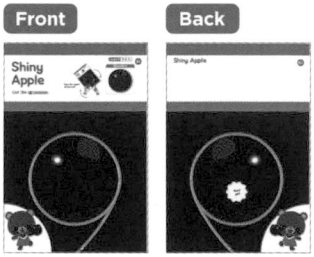

4) In order to handle scissors safely, it is important for parents and children to share the following rules: (1) Tell an adult before using scissors; (2) Always use scissors while sitting; (3) Don't use the scissors to point; (4) Don't cut anyone's hair, including your own or your pet's; (5) Hand the scissors to an adult when you are done using them.

5) When your child finishes each activity, let them choose a **reward sticker** to place on the page. Be sure to praise your child's good work! Be specific with your praise, saying something like, "You did a good job!" or "You were very patient!"

How to Hold Scissors

Insert your thumb into the smaller opening of the scissors. Then insert your index finger and middle finger (in some cases, your ring finger as well) into the larger opening.

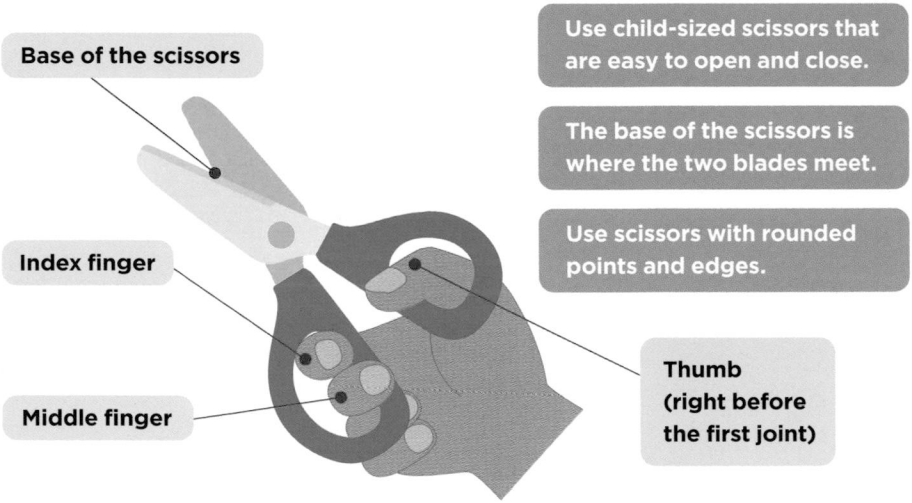

Use child-sized scissors that are easy to open and close.

The base of the scissors is where the two blades meet.

Use scissors with rounded points and edges.

How to Use Scissors

When using scissors, the elbow of the arm holding the scissors should be touching the body at the waist. Scissors should be held straight out from the body, and the paper should be held perpendicular to the scissors.

Hold the scissors in one hand and the paper in the other hand. Initially, it may be necessary for a parent to hold the paper.

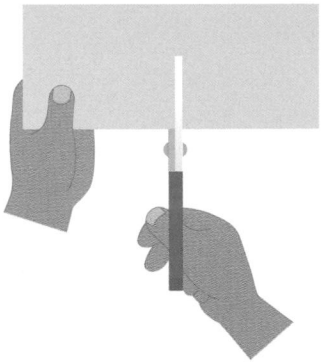

Insert the paper deep into the scissors. Open and partially close the blades repeatedly to cut a straight line.

Caution: The paper in this book can be sharp. Take care when handling. This book contains small stickers. Keep out of mouths. Be careful when using scissors, and use them only with an adult.

Reward Stickers

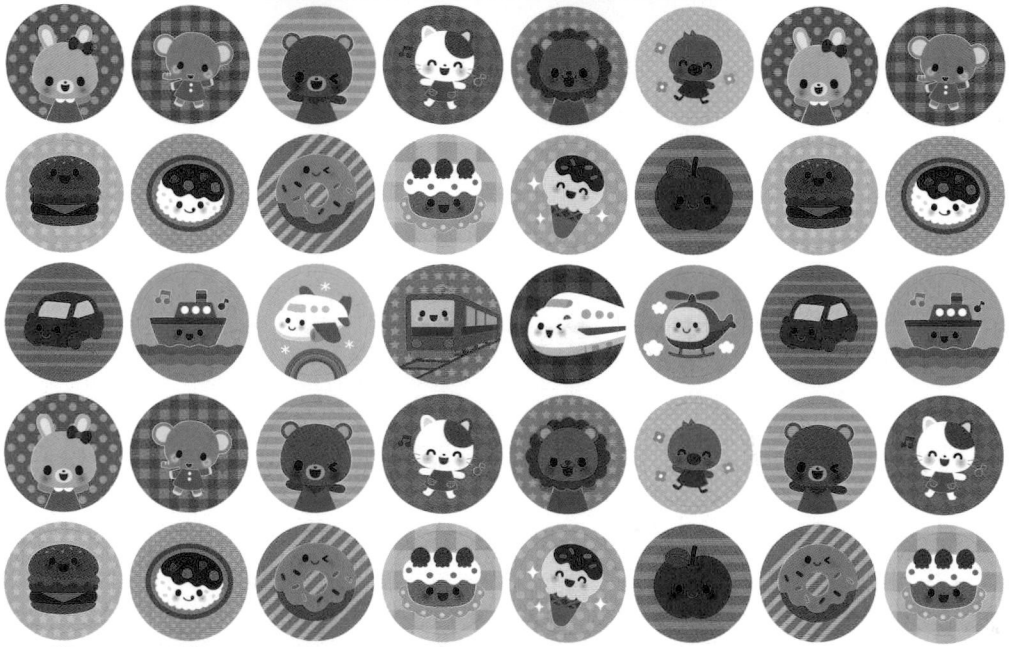

Activity Stickers (For pages 99, 101, 103, 125, 127)

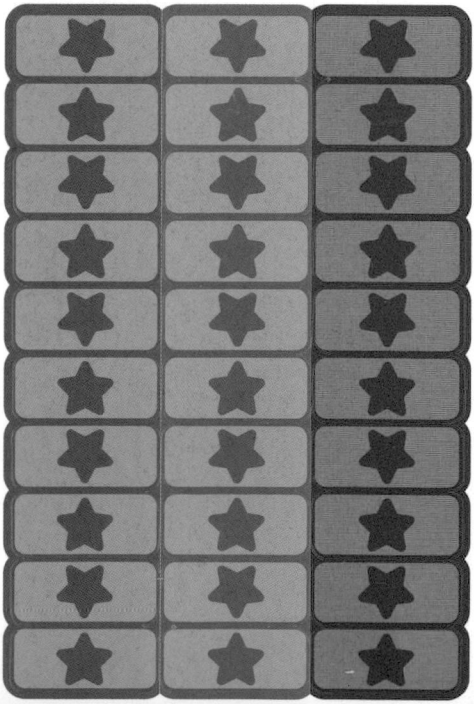

Level 1 ★☆☆

Water the Flowers

Example

Cut the ▭ into several pieces.
Put them on the picture to water the flowers.

To Parents While your child is getting used to cutting with scissors, place your hand over their hand to help guide them. Let them cut one "water" piece at a time while saying, "Let's water the flowers."

Parents: Cut this line for your child.

Water the Flowers

Parents: Cut the pink line. Your child can complete the rest of the activity.

Cut the water into several pieces.

Put the pieces on the picture to water the flowers.

Good job!

Level 1 ★☆☆

5

Flapping Penguin

Example

Cut the ✂ and fold on the - - - - - - - - to flap the penguin's wings.

Flapping Penguin

Tips for cutting horizontal lines.

It is difficult to use scissors to cut in a horizontal way.

Turn the paper so you can cut the line going straight out in front of you.

Peeka...

boo!

Play the Drums

Example

Cut the ✂ and fold on the - - - - - - - - to play the drums.

To Parents Cut the thick pink line first. Encourage your child to cut the two gray lines and fold on the dotted lines. Then let them make the cat play the drums.

Parents: Cut this line for your child.

Play the Drums

Parents: Cut the pink line. Your child can complete the rest of the activity.

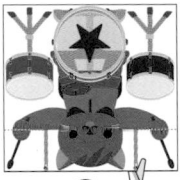

Turn the paper so your child can cut the gray lines vertically.

Rat-a-tat!

Good job!

Level 1 ★☆☆

Strawberry Cake

Example

Cut the along the .
Put the strawberries on the cake.

Cut out the pieces on the along the .
Put the strawberries on the cake.

Parents: Cut this line for your child.

Strawberry Cake

Parents: Cut the pink line. Your child can complete the rest of the activity.

Cut out each strawberry.

Put the strawberries on the cake.

Good job!

Play with Butterflies

Level 1 ★☆☆

Example

Cut out the pieces on the along the .
Put the butterflies on the picture and let them fly.

Parents: Cut this line for your child.

Play with Butterflies

Parents: Cut the pink line. Your child can complete the rest of the activity.

Cut out each butterfly.

Put the butterflies on the picture.

Good job!

Sea Animals

Cut out the pieces on the along the . Put the animals on the picture and let them swim.

Example

Parents: Cut this line for your child.

Sea Animals

Parents: Cut the pink line. Your child can complete the rest of the activity.

Cut out each sea animal.

Add the sea animals to the picture and let them swim.

Good job!

Level 2 ★★☆

15

Elephant Shower

Example

Cut the ✂ and fold on the - - - - - - - - to watch the elephant splash the kids.

To Parents Have your child practice cutting short lines. Your child should keep the scissors open and close them only slightly to make the cuts at the base of the scissors, without closing the scissors all the way.

Elephant Shower

Tips for cutting longer lines.

Don't completely close the scissors in the middle of the line.

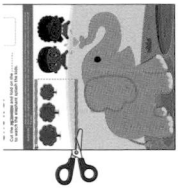

Close the scissors only halfway while cutting the line.

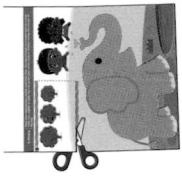

Reopen the scissors wide and continue cutting.

Fold the paper and watch the elephant splash the kids.

Good job!

Ice Cream Scoops

Example

Cut the ✂ and fold on the - - - - - - - - to put ice cream on the cone.

Ice Cream Scoops

Cut the gray line. Don't completely close the scissors while cutting.

Fold the paper to add ice cream scoops.

Here is your ice cream cone!

Good job!

Swinging Panda

Example

Cut the ✂ and fold on the ····· to see the baby panda swing in a tire.

To Parents After your child cuts the paper and folds on the dotted line, say "Swing, swing!" while closing and opening the paper.

Swinging Panda

Watch the playful baby panda swing in the tire.

Good job!

Cat Ears

Example

Cut the ✂ to give the cat ears.

To Parents When cutting diagonal lines, have your child position the paper so the line being cut is vertical. They should cut it as they would cut a straight line.

Cat Ears

Make different cats by changing the positions of the ears.

To Parents When your child places the triangles on the cat's head, let them know there are different ways to place them.

Good job!

House Puzzle

Cut the ✂ and match the pieces to make a window on the house.

Example

To Parents When your child is cutting a diagonal line, have them hold the paper close to the line with the hand that isn't holding the scissors. This will prevent the paper from shifting.

Parents: Cut this line for your child.

House Puzzle

Parents: Cut the pink line. Your child can complete the rest of the activity.

Match the puzzle pieces to make a window.

Level 1 ★☆☆

Bus Windows

Example

Cut the ✂ and put a friend in each window of the bus.

To Parents This activity practices cutting from two different directions to make a square. Ask your child to cut to where the lines cross.

Bus Windows

Tips for cutting corners.

Cut to the corner.

Turn the paper.

Cut to the corner again.

Put each friend on the bus.

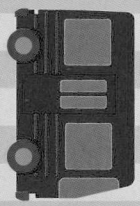

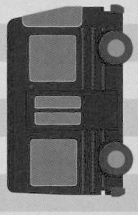

Toy Box

Cut the ✂ and fold on the - - - - - - - - to make a toy box.

Example

Parents: Cut this line for your child.

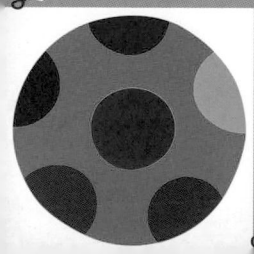

Toy Box

Parents: Cut the pink line. Your child can complete the rest of the activity.

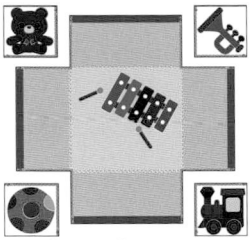

Cut out the corners.

Fold the paper to make a box.

Put a toy inside the box.

Good job!

Gentle Elephant

Level 2 ★★☆

Example

Cut the ✂ to make the elephant's trunk and legs swing.

To Parents Have your child practice cutting short and long lines. Your child should keep the scissors open and close them only slightly to make the cuts at the base of the scissors, without closing the scissors all the way.

Gentle Elephant

Watermelon Puzzle

Level 2 ★★☆

31

Example

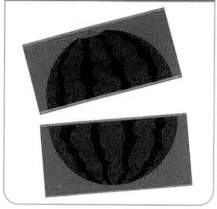

Cut the ✂ and combine the two pieces to make a round watermelon.

To Parents Your child can practice cutting long lines, which requires them to open and partially close the scissors repeatedly. But if your child has difficulty, cut halfway for them and let them cut the rest.

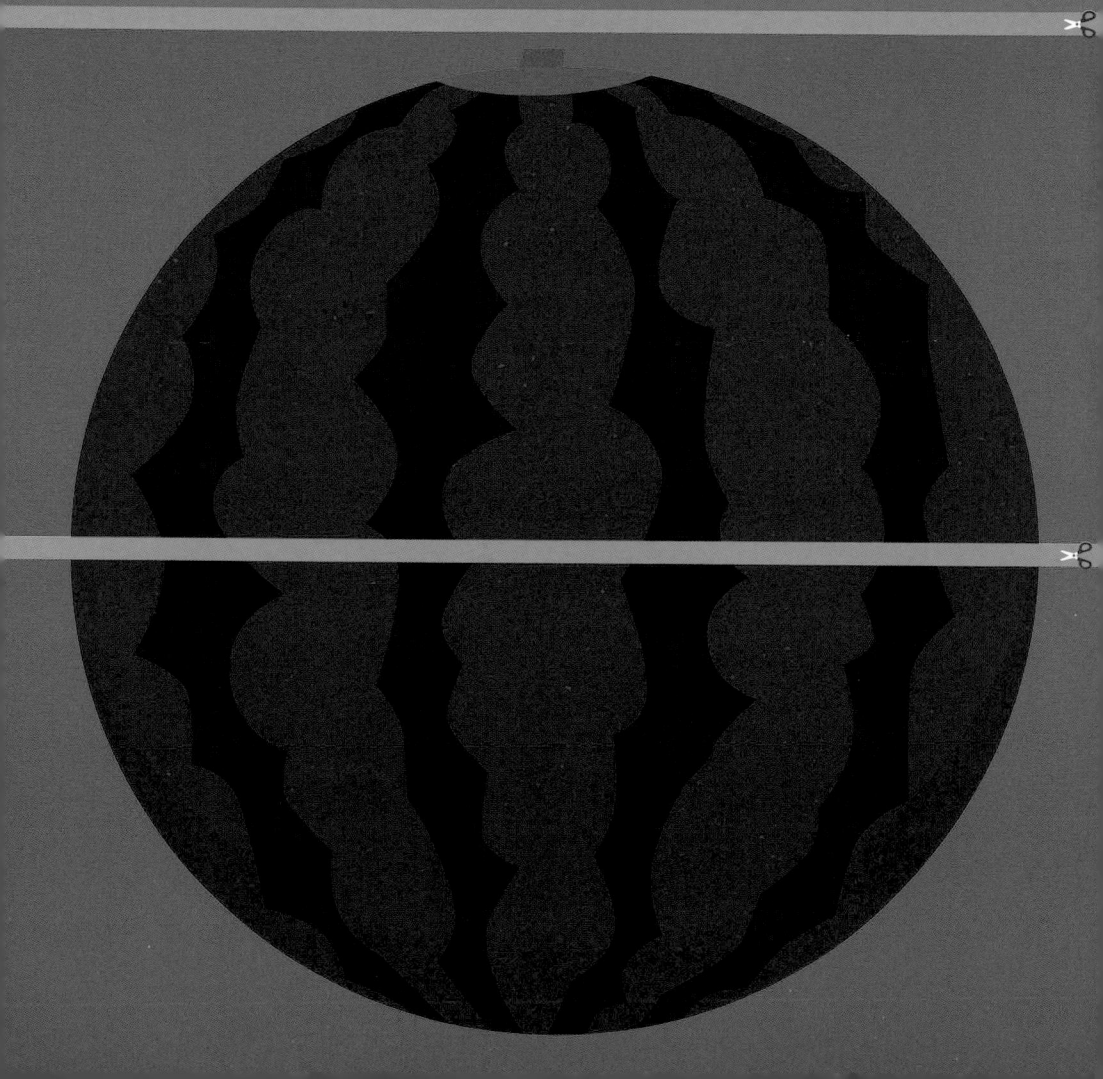

Watermelon Puzzle

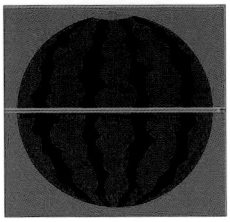

Front

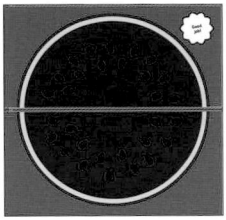

Back

Pretend to eat the juicy watermelon.

Good job!

Level 2 ★★☆

33

Tower Puzzle

Example

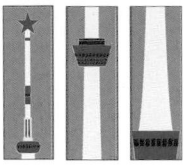

Cut the ✂ to make a soaring tower.

To Parents If this is difficult for your child, show them how to cut by keeping the scissors open and closing them only slightly to make cuts at the base of the scissors, without closing the scissors all the way.

Parents: Cut this line for your child.

Tower Puzzle

Parents: Cut the pink line. Your child can complete the rest of the activity.

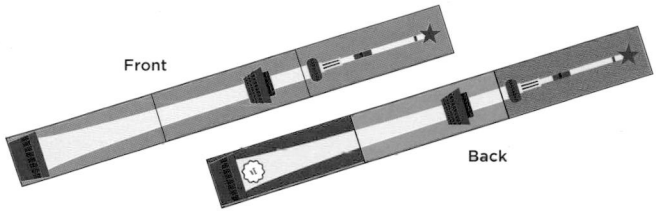

Good job!

Melon Puzzle

Example

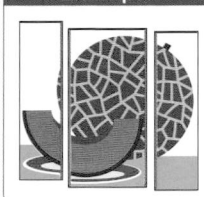

Cut the ✂ and combine the three pieces to make a picture.

To Parents For this activity, your child will form a picture with the three puzzle pieces. Both sides of the pieces are identical, so either side may be used to complete the puzzle.

Parents: Cut this line for your child.

Melon Puzzle

Parents: Cut the pink line. Your child can complete the rest of the activity.

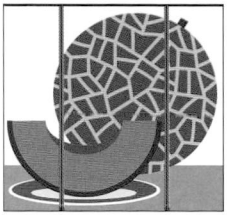

Front

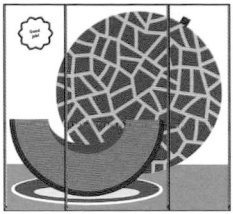

Back

Train Puzzle

Cut the ✂ and combine the three pieces to make a speedy train.

Example

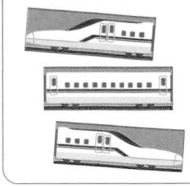

To Parents In this activity, your child can line up the three puzzle pieces to form a long train. The pieces on the back side of this page can be rearranged to form a different train.

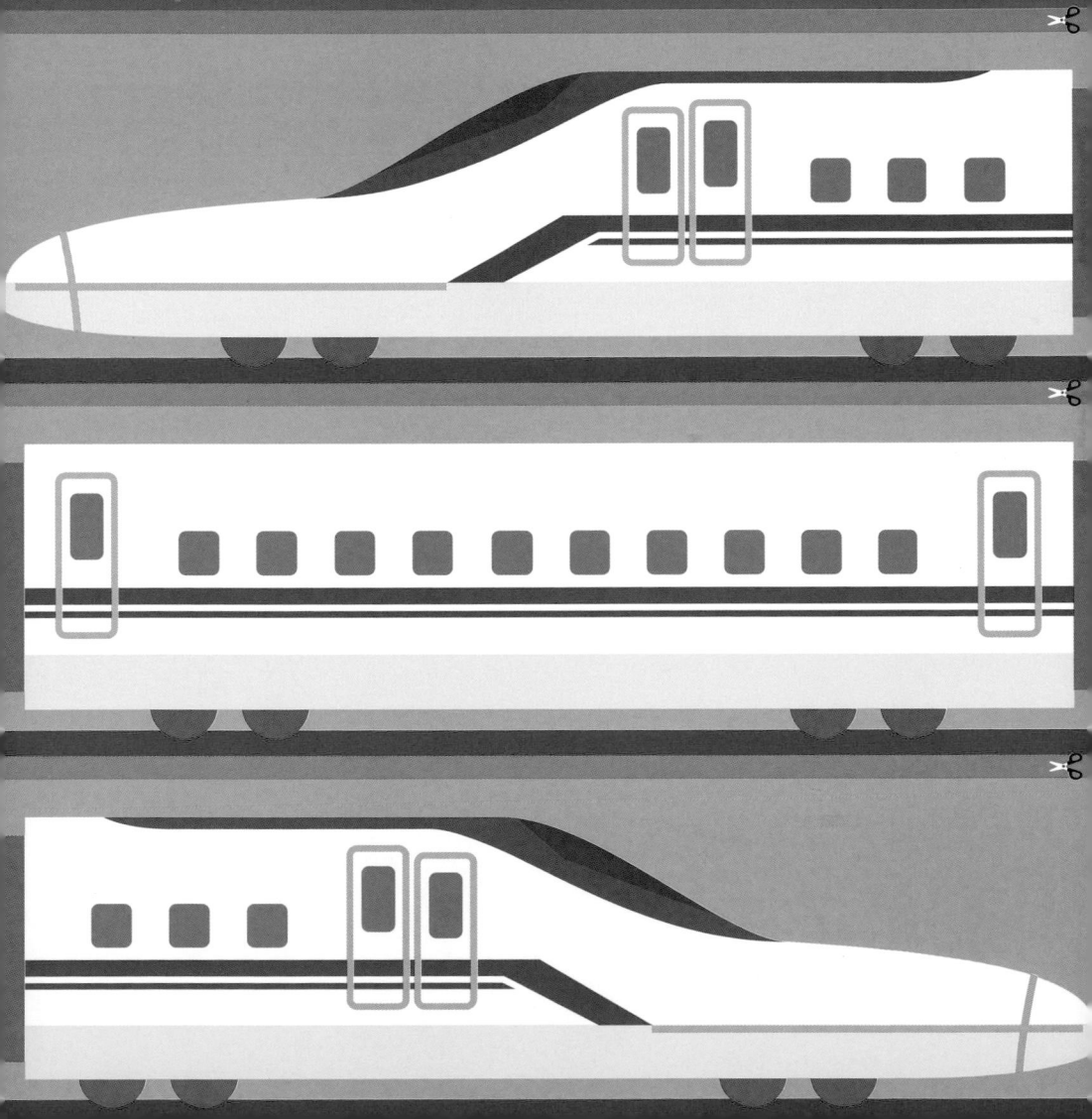

Train Puzzle

Front

Back

Good job!

Level 2 ★★☆

39

Hot Pizza

Example

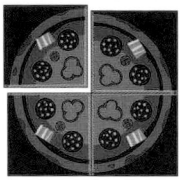

Cut the ✂ and combine the four pieces to make a round pizza.

To Parents Don't worry if your child cuts off the line. Just give them lots of praise for using the scissors to cut.

Parents: Cut this line for your child.

Hot Pizza

Parents: Cut the pink line. Your child can complete the rest of the activity.

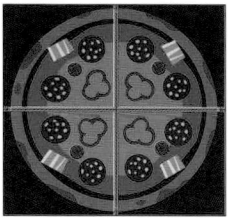

Front

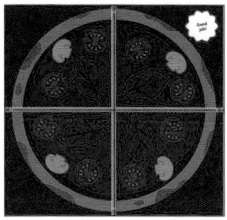

Back

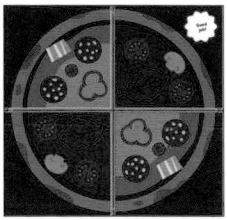

Combination

Level 3 ★★★

41

Juicy Watermelon

Cut the ✂ .

Example

To Parents Curved lines should be cut by turning the paper to keep the line vertical to your body, not by moving the scissors in the direction of the line. Show your child an example.

Turn the paper.

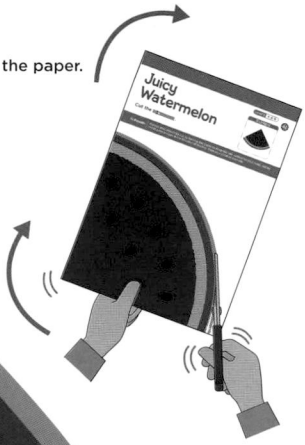

Hold scissors straight in front of you, and move them calmly and slowly.

Juicy Watermelon

Pretend to eat a juicy slice of watermelon.

Good job!

Level 3 ★★★

43

Yellow Bananas

Example

Cut the ✂ .

Yellow Bananas

Level 3 ★★★

Mighty Dinosaur

Example

Cut the ✂ .

To Parents This activity focuses on cutting a reverse S-shape line. As this can be difficult, encourage your child to cut a little at a time while slowly shifting the position of the paper.

Mighty Dinosaur

Level 3 ★★★

47

Wiggly Octopus

Example

Cut the ✂.

To Parents Have your child cut the paper while turning it. If this is difficult because the octopus is surrounded by paper, roughly cut it out before giving it to your child.

Wiggly Octopus

Colorful Umbrella

Level 3 ★★★

Example

Cut the ✂ .

To Parents After they cut one line, let your child change the position of the paper so the line to be cut is vertical to their body.

Colorful Umbrella

Car Ride

Cut the ✂ .

Example

To Parents To be able to stop cutting at the corner, your child should practice making short cuts only at the base of the scissors until they reach the end of the line.

Car Ride

King's Crown

Cut the ✂.

Example

To Parents Once your child is comfortable with the scissors, let them try to do it without your help. When they are able to do it on their own, praise them for a job well done.

King's Crown

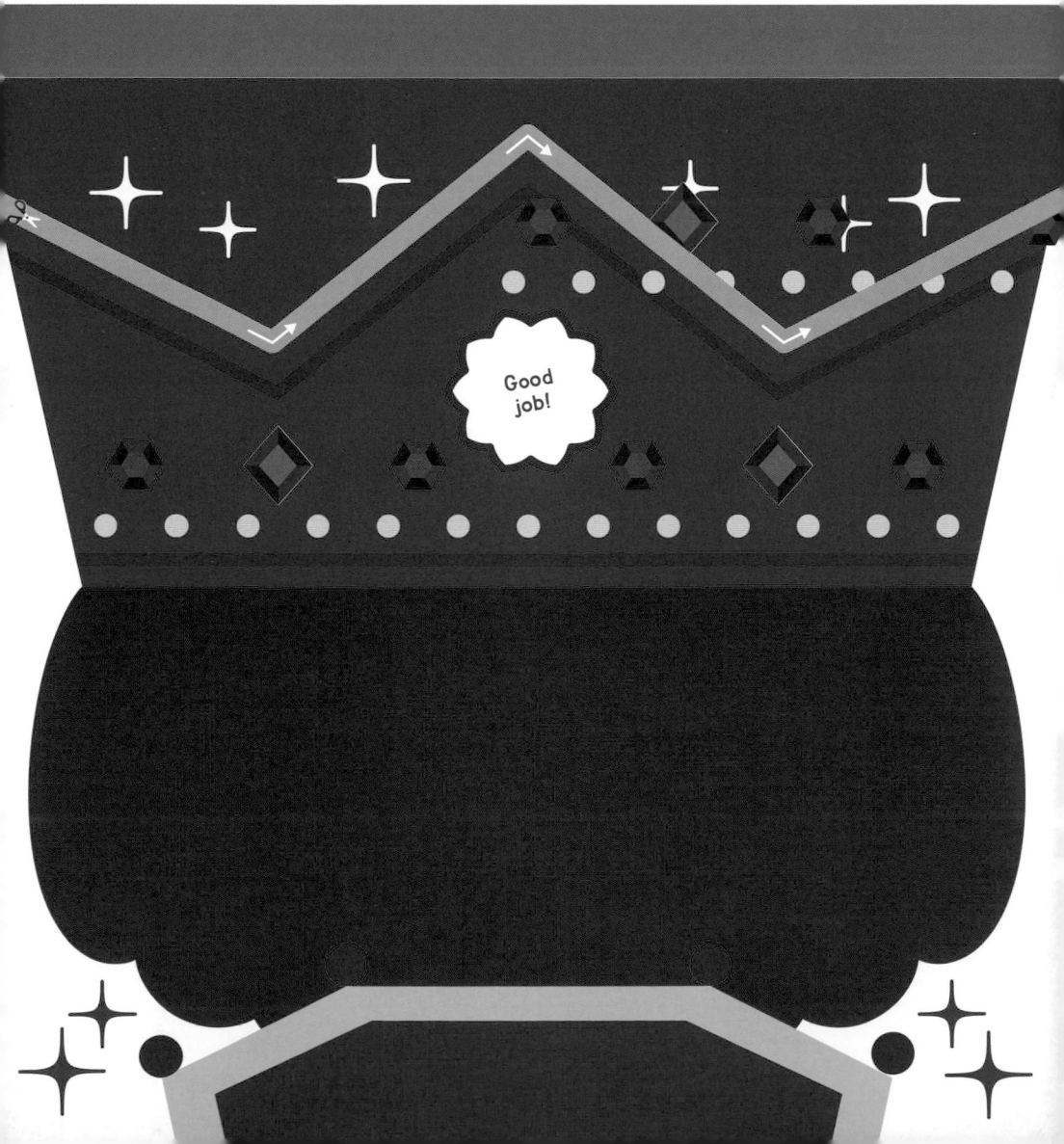

Blue Bird

Cut the ✂ .

Example

Blue Bird

Happy Bunny

Cut the ✂ .

Example

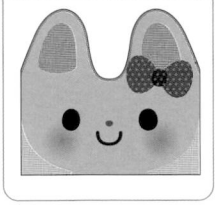

Happy Bunny

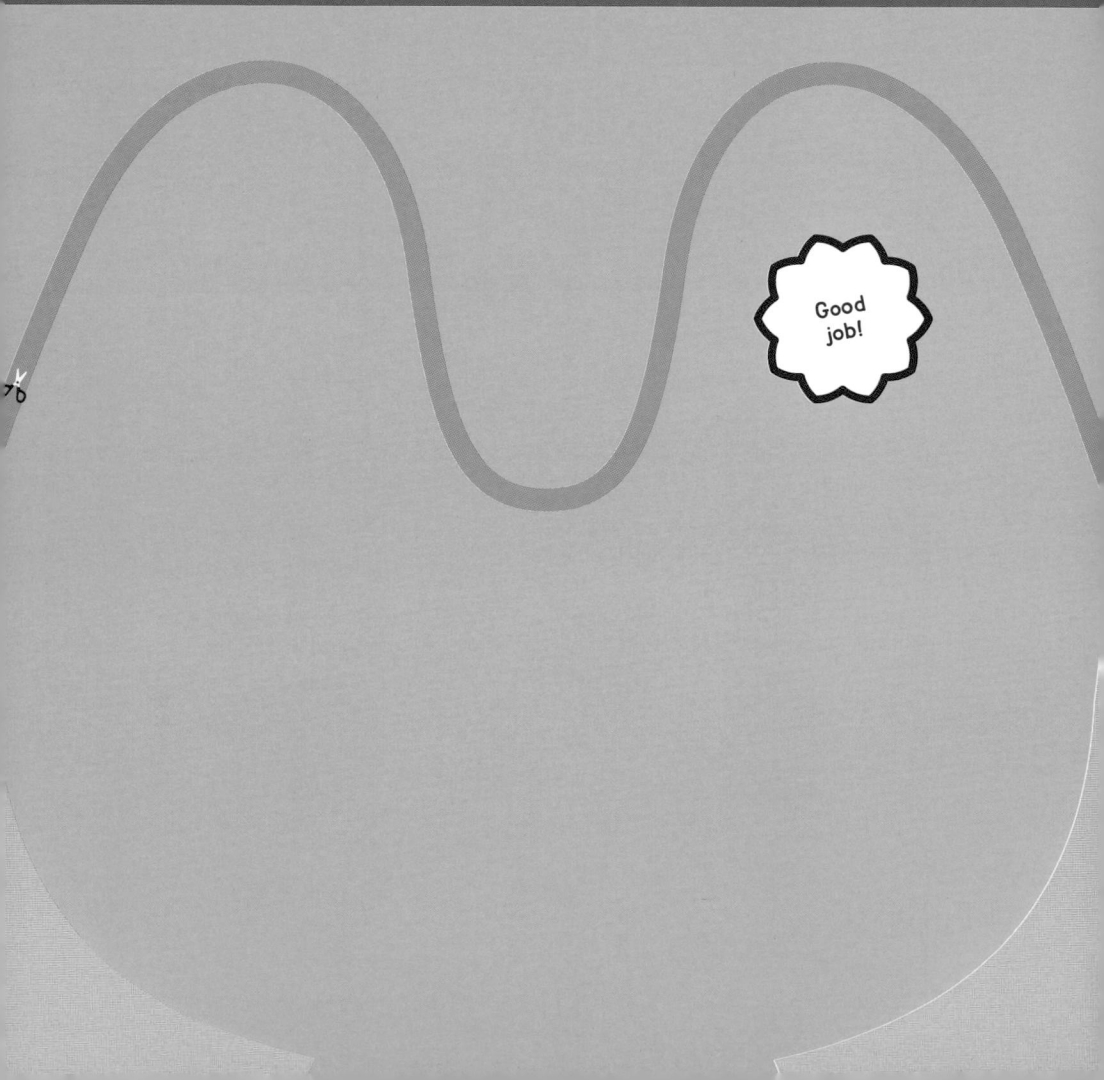

Flying Butterfly

Level 3 ★★★

Example

Cut the ✂ and make the butterfly flutter.

To Parents When your child gets to a corner, let them turn the paper around and start cutting again. Show them where to stop cutting so you can shift the paper.

Flying Butterfly

Hold the center of the butterfly to flutter its wings.

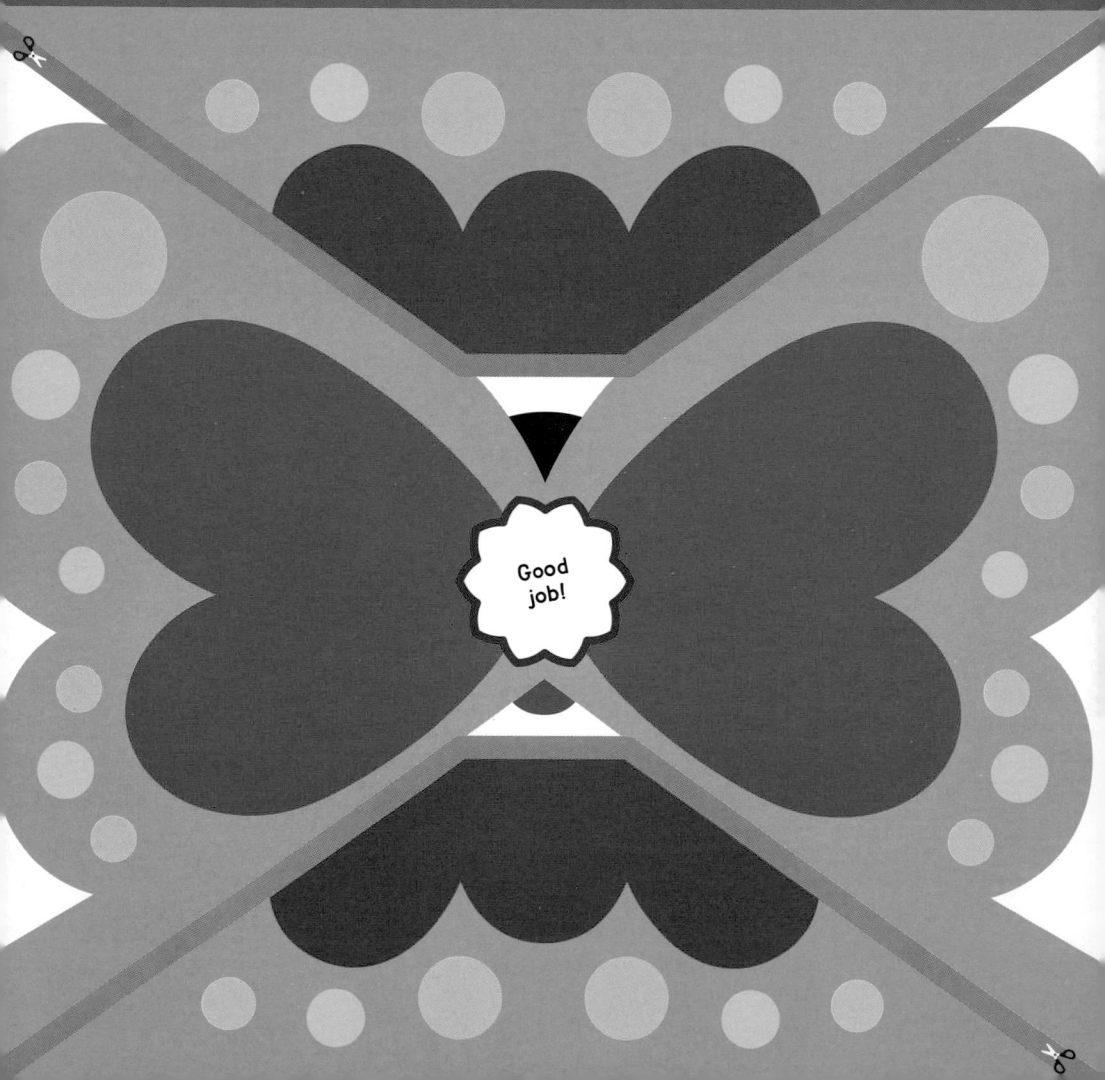

Shiny Apple

Cut the ✂ .

Turn the paper as you cut.

Example

Shiny Apple

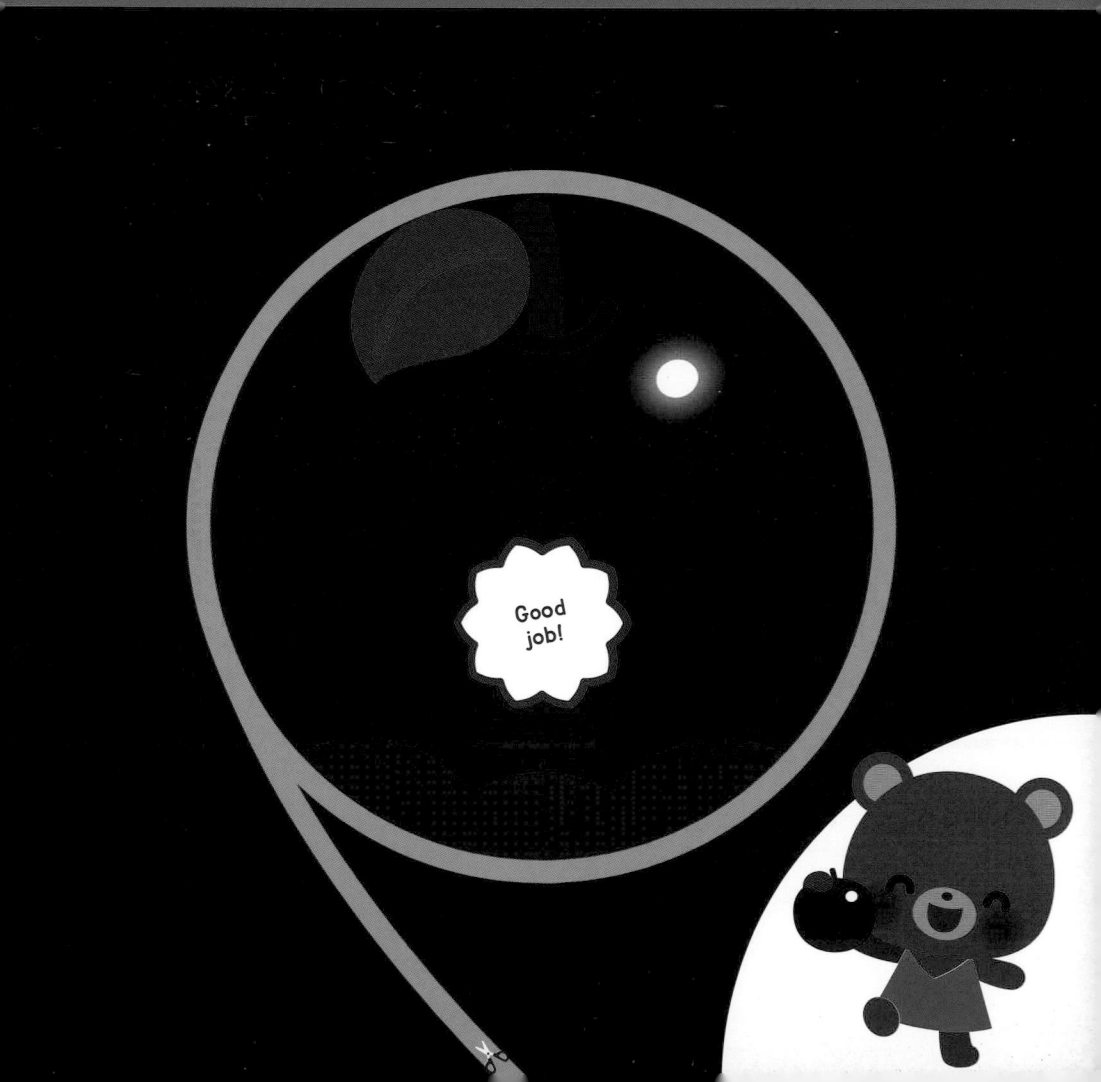

Level 3 ★★★

63

Swimming Dolphin

Example

Cut the ✂ and fold on the - - - - - - - - to make the dolphin swim.

Swimming Dolphin

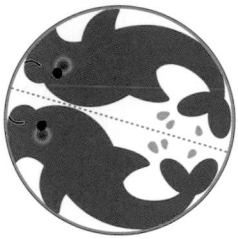

Good job!

Walking Dog

Cut the ✂ and make the dog walk.

Example

Walking Dog

Toy Closet

Example

Cut the ✂ and fold on the ····· to open and close the closet doors.

To Parents Have your child fold the paper on the dotted lines. Then, open and close the closet doors. Ask them, "What's in there?" and "Where's the ball?"

Toy Closet

Good job!

Apple Tree

Example

Cut out the pieces on the along the . Put apples on the tree.

To Parents Cut the pink line and then hand the strip of paper to your child. Have your child hold it in one hand and cut off each piece, starting from the side with the scissors.

Parents: Cut this line for your child.

Apple Tree

Parents: Cut the pink line. Your child can complete the rest of the activity.

Cut out the apples.

Put the apples on the tree.

Good job!

Flower Garden

Example

Cut out the pieces on the along the . Put flowers in the garden.

Parents: Cut this line for your child.

Flower Garden

Parents: Cut the pink line. Your child can complete the rest of the activity.

Cut out the flowers.

Put the flowers in the garden.

Good job!

Reach High

Cut the ✂ and fold on the - - - - - - - -.
Then fold each flap up.

To Parents When the paper is cut and folded, your child can enjoy changing the picture. When the picture is changed, say to your child, "The hat blew off!" or "The dinosaur saved the hat!"

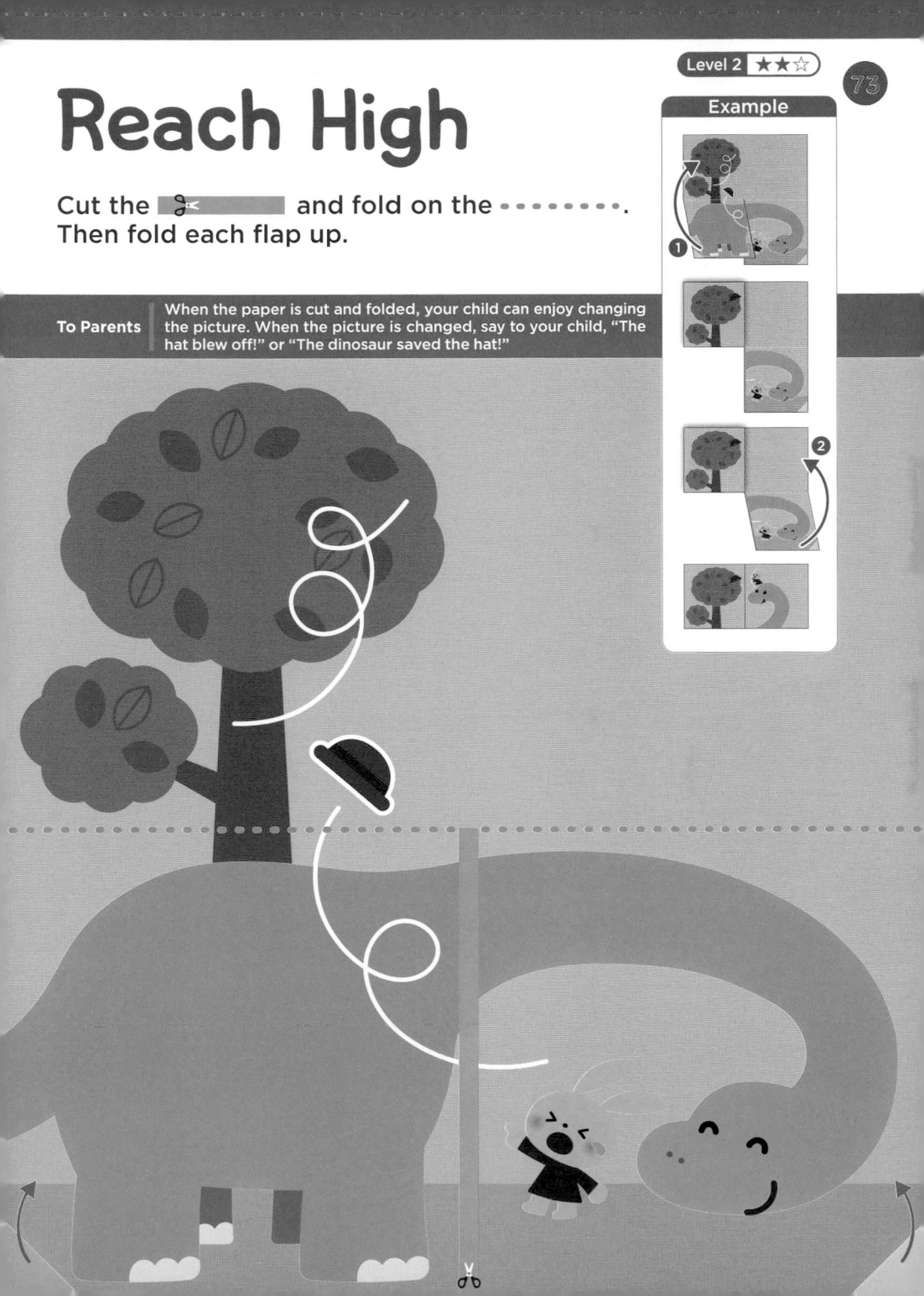

Good job!

Pink Pig

Cut the ✂ and put the pig's ears, nose, and mouth on the face.

Example

Parents: Cut this line for your child.

Pink Pig

Parents: Cut the pink line. Your child can complete the rest of the activity.

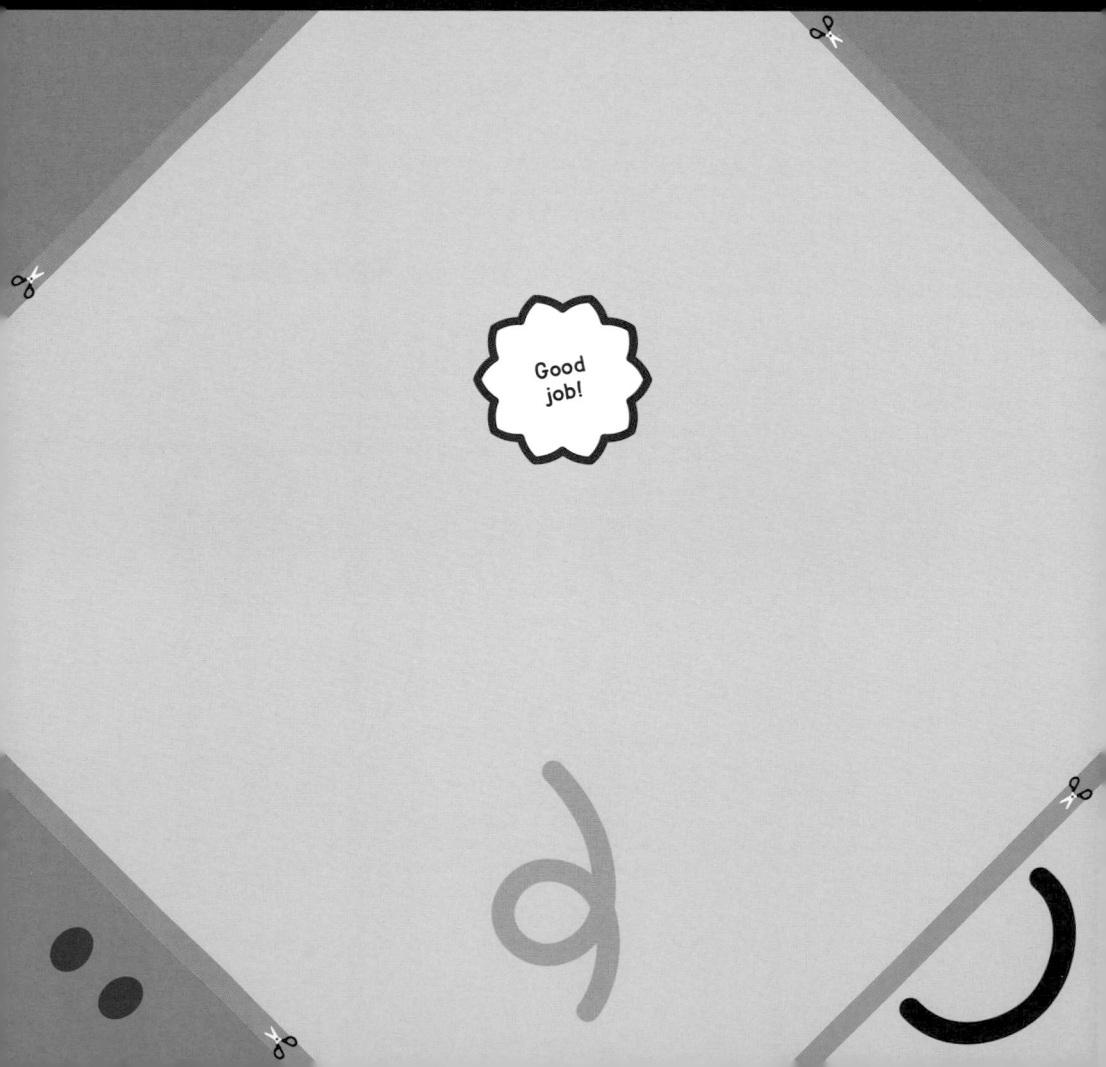

Level 1 ★☆☆

77

Kitchen Table

Cut the ✂ and fold the paper on the - - - - - - - - to add food to the table.

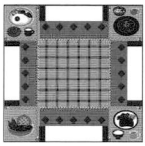

Example

Parents: Cut this line for your child.

Kitchen Table

Parents: Cut the pink line. Your child can complete the rest of the activity.

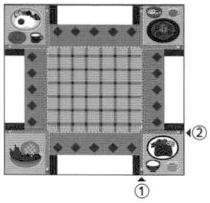

Cut each corner from opposite directions.

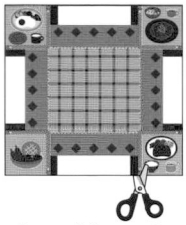

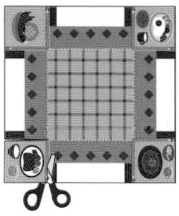

Cut each line to the corner. Turn the paper and cut the other line to the corner.

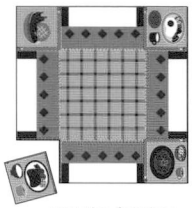

Put the food on the table.

Get Dressed

Cut the ✂ to put clothes on the boy and girl.

Example

To Parents This activity focuses on cutting short horizontal and vertical lines. Your child's scissors should always be pointed away from the body. Have them cut a vertical line, then turn the paper so the next line being cut is vertical, and cut to where the first one ended.

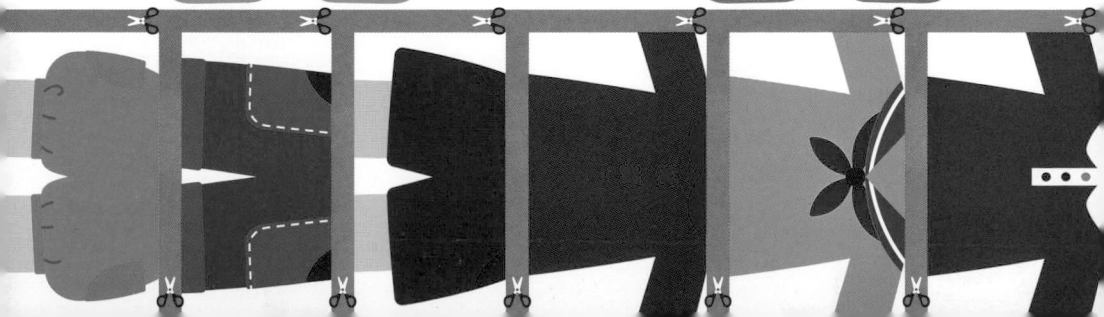

Get Dressed

Tips for cutting individual pieces.

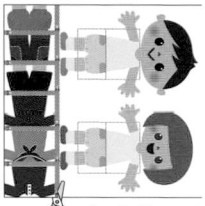

Cut halfway along the gray line.

Turn the paper, then cut to where the last cut ended.

Put the clothes on the kids.

Elephant and Giraffe

Example

Cut the ✂ and fold on the - - - - - - - - to make the elephant and giraffe stand.

To Parents If your child completely closes the scissors each time they cut a long line, the paper will be jagged. Encourage your child to continue cutting while opening and partially closing the scissors with small cuts. Repeat these actions.

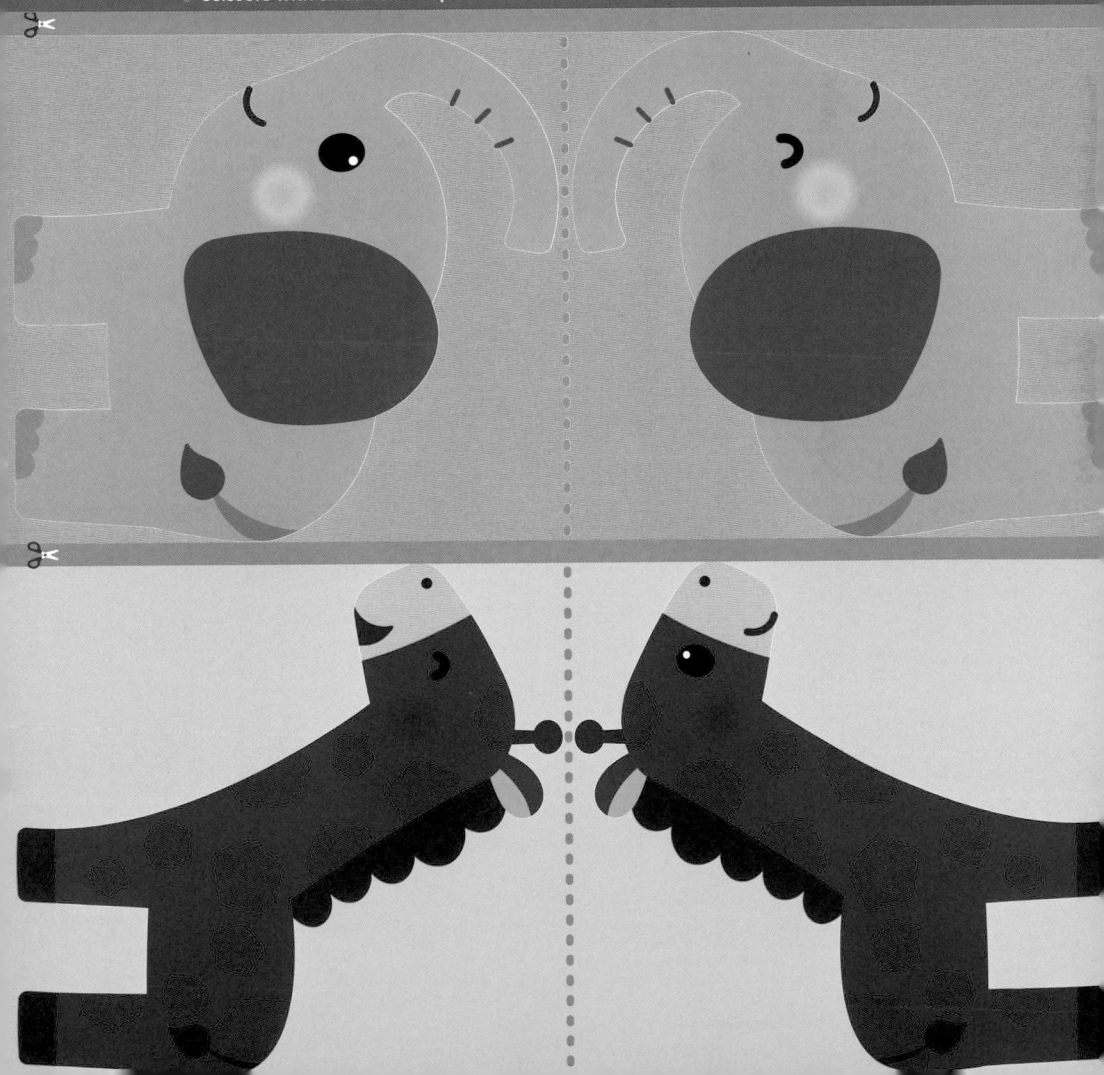

Elephant and Giraffe

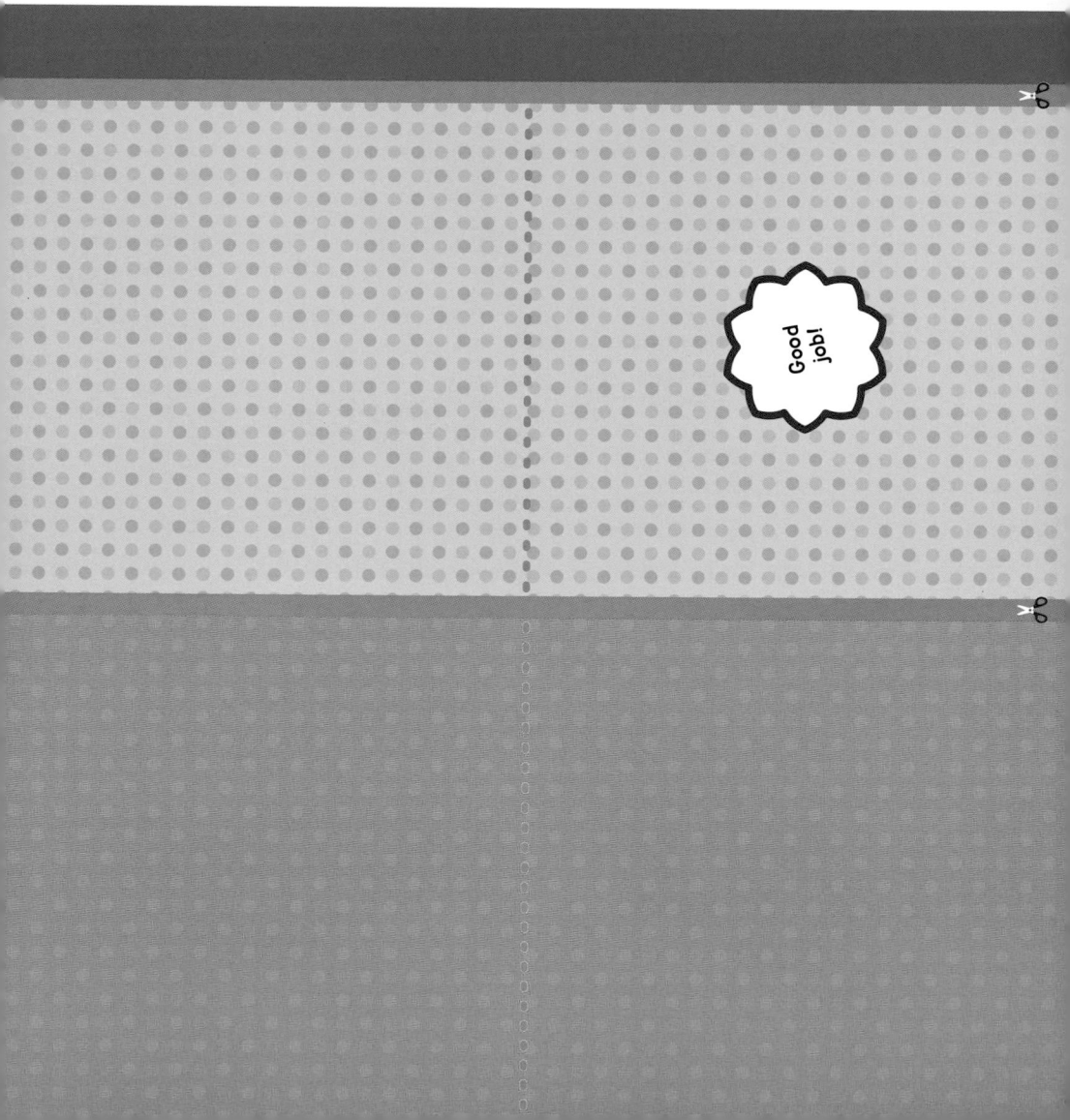

Sled Race

First cut the ✂ ▬▬▬▬▬▬▬▬.
Then cut the ✂ ▬▬▬▬▬▬▬▬.
Fold the paper on the - - - - - - - - to make the sleds stand.

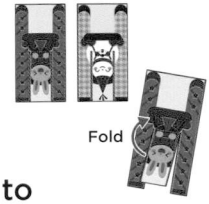

Example

To Parents This activity practices cutting to the end of the line without cutting off the paper. When your child is close to the end of the line, have them cut a little at a time, stopping at the right position.

Parents: Cut this line for your child.

Sled Race

Parents: Cut the pink line. Your child can complete the rest of the activity.

Place the finished work on the desk and try to move it by blowing.

Slithering Snake

First cut the .
Then cut the .

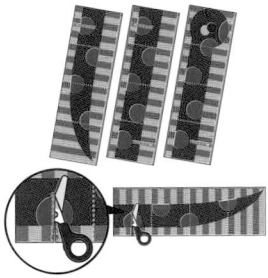

Example

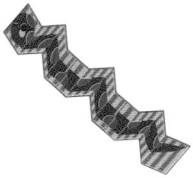

To Parents Show your child how to fold the paper in a zigzag pattern.

Slithering Snake

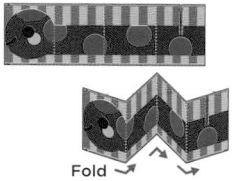

Fold the paper on the - - - - - to make a wiggly snake.

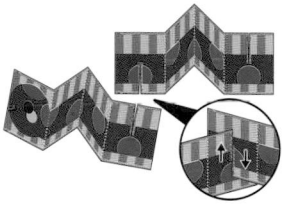

Insert one notch into another to combine the pieces.

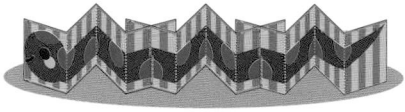

Make the slithering snake longer.

Good job!

Fast Vehicles

First cut the ✂. Then cut the ✂. Fold the paper on the ····· to make the vehicles stand.

Example

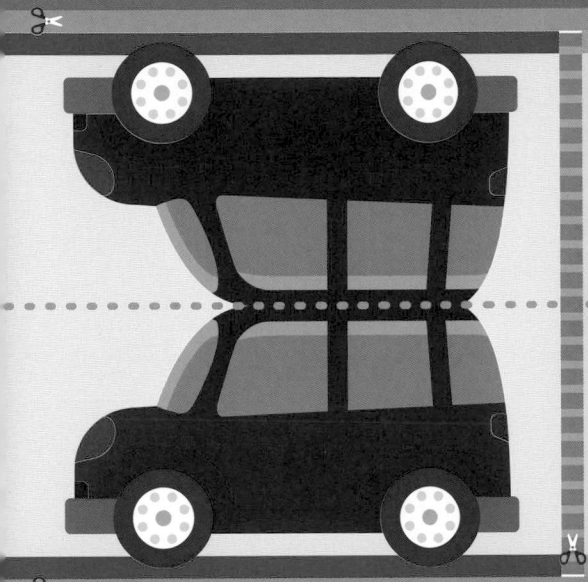

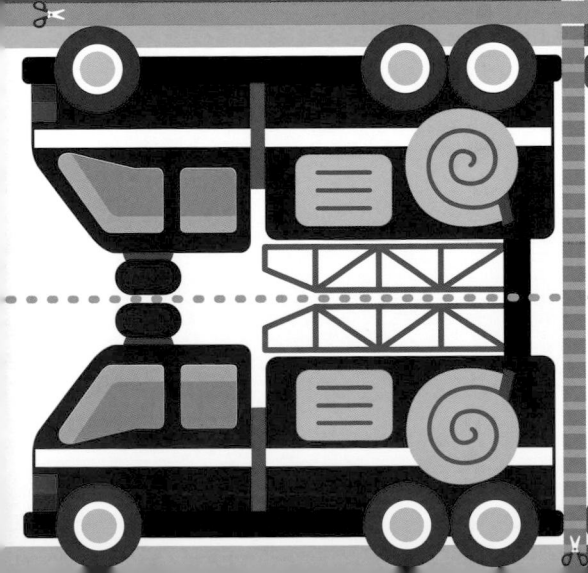

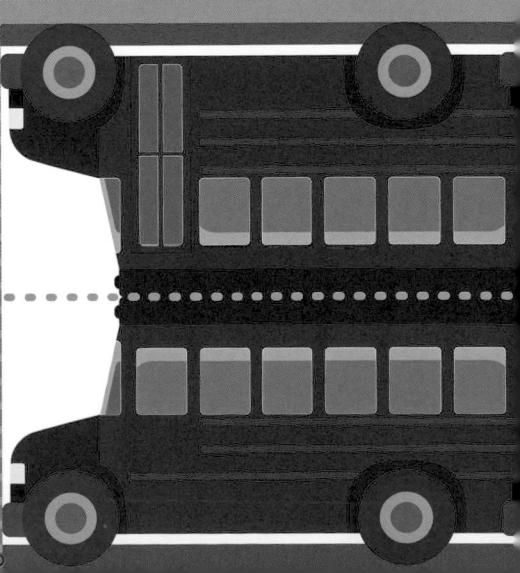

Fast Vehicles

Zooming Airplane

Example

Cut the ✂ .

To Parents If this is difficult for your child, roughly cut it out before giving it to them.

Zooming Airplane

Finger Puppets

Cut the first, then the and finally the .

☆See the back side of this page for further instructions.

Example

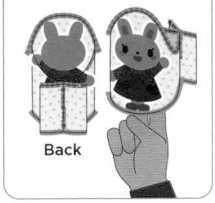

To Parents This activity practices cutting both straight and curved lines. After your child finishes cutting, have them fold the paper into a cylinder to make a finger puppet.

Finger Puppets

Cut along the ✂.

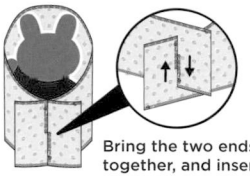

Bring the two ends together, and insert one notch into the other.

Play with your new finger puppet friend!

Good job!

Roller Coaster

Cut the ✂ .

Example

Roller Coaster

Gliding Sailboat

Example

Cut the ✂.

To Parents This yacht has many corners. Have your child cut while moving the position of the paper, not the scissors, when they need to change direction.

Gliding Sailboat

Ticking Clock

Cut the ✂.

Example

Ticking Clock

Floating Sea Otter

Fold the paper on the - - - - - - - and attach the stickers.
Place the sticker on the back side of this page, then cut the ✂.

Activity sticker

Example

To Parents This activity focuses on folding the paper and cutting while it's overlapped. When your child is finished, make the sea otter swing back and forth.

Place sticker here

Place sticker here

Place sticker here

Floating Sea Otter

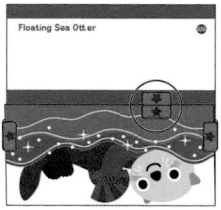

After folding the paper, put the sticker on this side.

This side

Good job!

Flying Balloon

Example

Place sticker here

Fold the paper on the - - - - - - - - and attach the stickers.
Cut the ✂ ▬▬▬▬.

To Parents Tell your child to fold, sticker, and cut in that order.

Place sticker here

Place sticker here

Flying Balloon

Ice Cream Swirl

Fold the paper on the - - - - - - - -
and attach the stickers.
Cut the ✂ .

Example

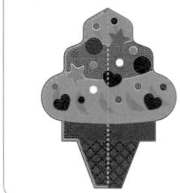

Place sticker here

Place sticker here

Place sticker here

Ice Cream Swirl

Birthday Cake

Example

Cut the ✂.

Birthday Cake

Heart Card

Cut the ✂ .

Example

Heart Card

Good job!

LOVE

Yummy Strawberry

Cut the ✂.

Example

Yummy Strawberry

Sweet Bananas

Example

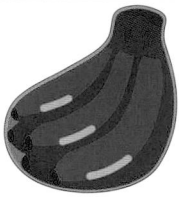

Cut the ✂.

Sweet Bananas

Flower Fairy

Example

Cut the ✂ and pick up the Flower Fairy.

To Parents Cutting a spiral line is similar to cutting a circle. Because the paper must be turned as your child cuts, encourage your child to move the position of the paper, not the scissors, as they go.

Flower Fairy

Good job!

Soaring Rocket

Example

Cut the ✂ and pick up the rocket.

To Parents Have your child rotate the paper, not the scissors, when the line changes direction, then continue cutting.

Soaring Rocket

Good job!

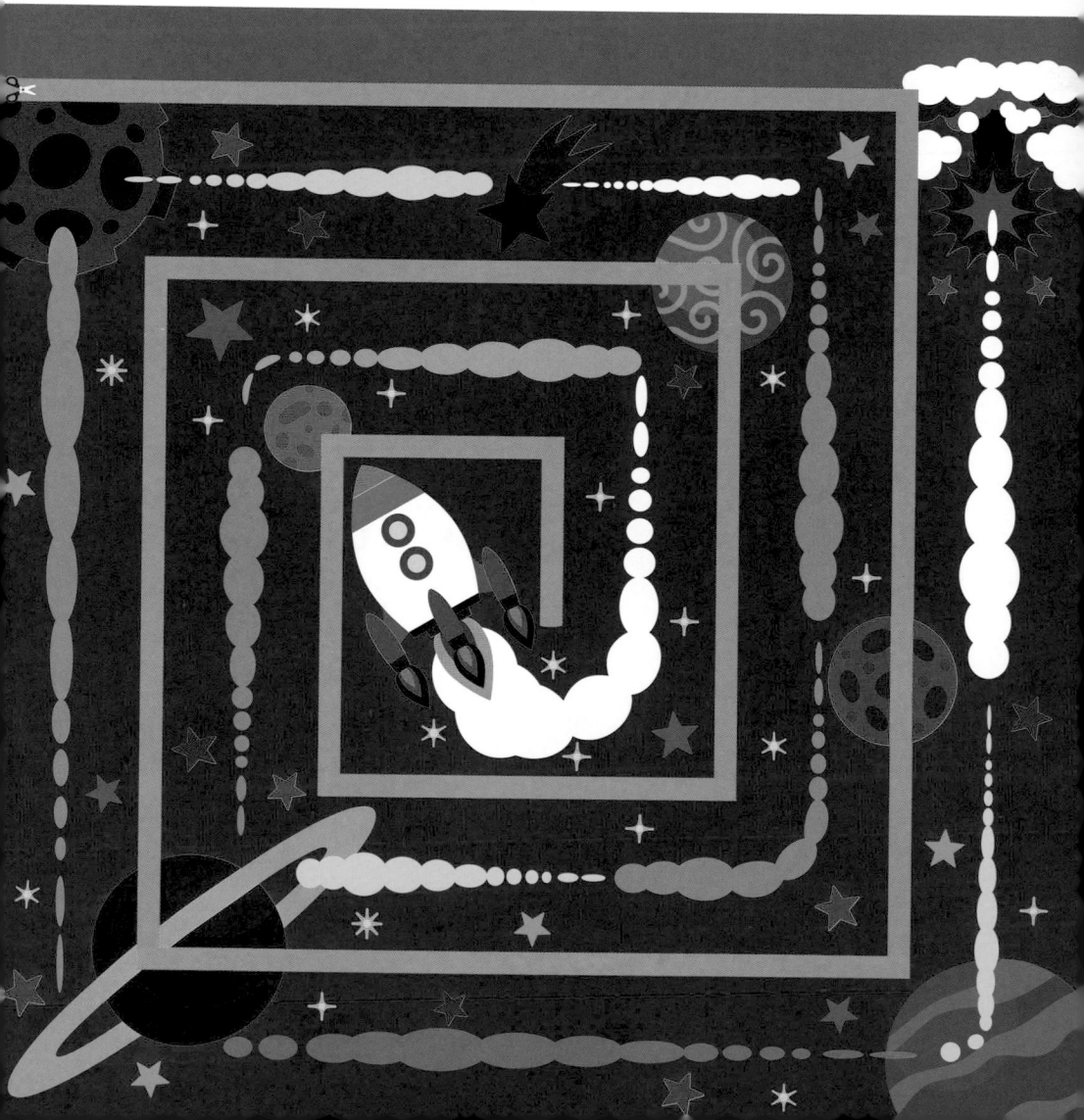

Spiral Snake

Cut the ✂ and pick up the snake.

Example

To Parents After your child cuts out the snake, pick up its head and shake it.

Spiral Snake

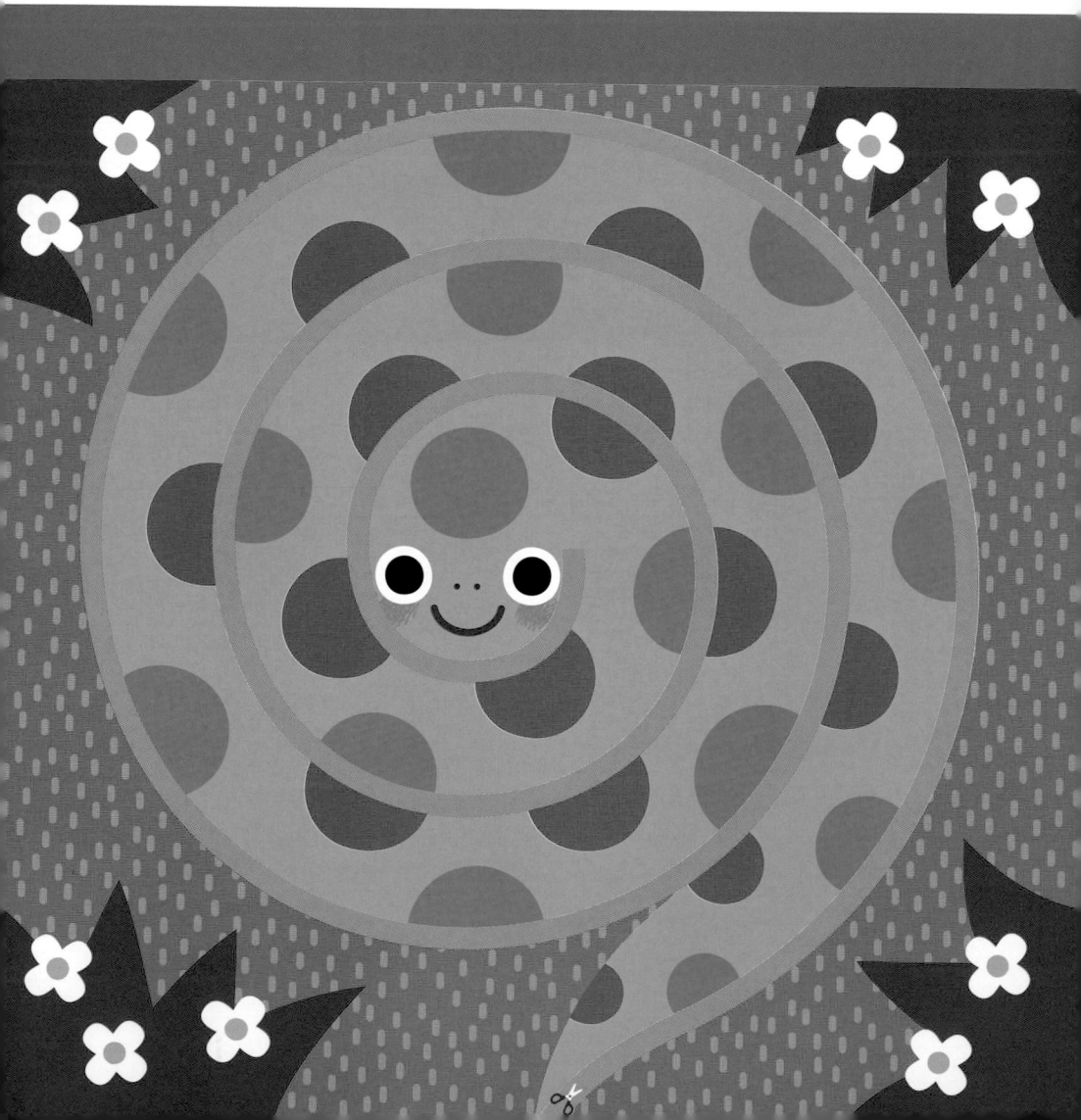

Funny Panda

Example

Cut the ✂.

To Parents Your child has successfully completed many activities throughout this book. They have practiced cutting and continue to improve. As your child cuts the panda's ears, have them cut while moving the position of the paper, not the scissors.

Funny Panda

Fuzzy Cat

Cut the ✂ .

Example

Fuzzy Cat

Beautiful Fish

Cut the ✂ .

Example

Beautiful Fish

Flying Bird

Level 3 ★★★

Fold the paper on the - - - - - - - -
and attach the two sides together
with the stickers.
Also place the sticker on the back
side of this page, then cut the
✂ .

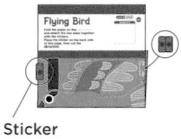

Example

Place sticker here

Place sticker here

Place sticker here

Flying Bird

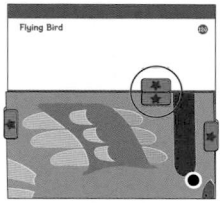

After folding, put a sticker on this side of the paper.

This side

Good job!

Talking Frog

Fold the paper along the - - - - - - - - and attach the sides together with the stickers. Cut the paper after folding it.

Example

To Parents This is a complicated shape, but have your child cut, following the rule of moving the paper and not the scissors.

Place sticker here

Place sticker here

Talking Frog

Hold the frog's cheeks.
Make it speak by opening
and closing its mouth.

Good job!